FOREWARD

In 2008 or 2009 I was intro┅ Facebook. Immediately a who┅ I was virtually connected to h┅ childhood friends, and nev┅ started networking and sharir┅ ┅┅┅ immediately highlighted a gift I was aware of which had been laying dormant for years. I've always loved the art of language, I was blessed with not only the gift of gab but the ability to put into words the things that others were feeling. I wrote love letters to girls for my friends, wrote papers for others that struggled and passed every English test I've ever took with a certain ease. In fact, in my high school back in Jamaica, I achieved the highest grades on a nationally graded test. I say all of this to say that I have always been aware of my gift with words. The problem with natural born talents is that because they usually come without effort, the bearer usually doesn't consider it an actual gift.

On Facebook, I quickly began to notice a trend of people posting positive quotes daily on their timelines and I decided to start doing this as well. I started sharing my thoughts each morning within the confines of the limited text space allowed. I began to notice that those on my friends list would consistently like and comment on my posts on a daily basis. They would tell me how much my words resonated with them and whenever I would take a day off, I would be flooded with messages of concern and requests for more posts.

As a kid growing up in Kingston Jamaica, I was groomed in the church and I remember a Sunday school teacher telling me I should be specific in what I prayed for and not to be selfish in my request to God. I remember coming up with a prayer specifically asking God for wisdom, knowledge and upstanding not realizing that one would have to go through major struggles in life to achieve those goals. My life over the years has allowed me to attain some unique life experiences that have shaped the way I look at the world.

I truly hope this book will serve as a source of daily inspiration to anyone who reads it, I can't take credit for the gift but through Facebook I've come to realize that my words which I normally take for granted can indeed be helpful to others. Thanks for sharing in my journey to becoming my best self. Bless

1

If you can make life exactly how you want it, it still wouldn't be perfect. No matter how hard you try to create a plan for your life, the unexpected will occur. If things don't happen exactly as you planned it, who can you really be angry at? This is life, so shouldn't you be prepared for its endless possibilities?

There is a certain joy that comes in realistically adjusting your expectations to achieve your end results. Life is what you make it only if you decide to take it all in stride.

_____

_____

_____

_____

_____

2

Be mindful that sometimes the good you do for yourself can still cause others pain. Always know why you do the things you do, as there might be times when your reason for doing what is right is the only comfort you will have. Others may judge your actions wrongfully based on how it affects them; just always make sure you're clear in the decisions you make, as they are connected to those who care about you.

_____

_____

_____

_____

_____

3

Don't worry if you're confused about life: it's the norm. There are many of us who are also clueless but continue to exist. One of the keys is the willingness to adjust and making sure you're doing more good than bad. Not having all the answers is no reason to stop. Continue moving while operating under the guidelines of love. Your heart will know, but your mind will confuse you creating actions contradictory to your feelings.

It's all life just continue living.

_____

_____

_____

_____

_____

4

If you've never challenged what you were taught, then you're truly missing out on one of life's greatest pleasures. Independent thinking promotes progress. Your world changes when you become brave enough not to accept what you find unsettling. Challenge it all until you're fully confident in the results of your search.

Just because it's widely accepted by many doesn't make it right.

_____

_____

_____

_____

_____

5

Things can happen that will challenge your belief in humanity, but you must never lose hope. What kind of life can you be living when at your core you don't believe "good" exists anymore? If you truly can't find any good to believe in, then you're part of the reason for this gloomy, pessimistic world. Regardless of your daily struggles, try to find something good to hold on to

The world needs more positive energy, so do your part.

6

Our insecurities can get the better of us at times. We end up going into certain situations believing we're not good enough, which leads to failure before we even start. The things we are insecure about are often not even recognizable by others until we introduce them as our reality. We are our worst enemy when we damage our confidence with false evidence.

The truth is, not only are we good enough, but we are on an equal level as the other humans we believe ourselves to be less than.

_____

_____

_____

_____

_____

7

When was the last time you freely gave to the world, what you expect from it daily? Often times what we receive, is simply a reflection of what we give out. It's unfair to selfishly expect good from others, when your actions lack the good your desire.

8

If it's not what you're called but what you answer to, then why do we worry so much about what others say about us? Most of us are so petrified of the labels other put on us that we live our lives according to their expectations. Live a free life and do what makes you happy.

_____

_____

_____

_____

_____

9

Regardless of what you're going through in life, you're still able to help others, even if it's just with a listening ear. You'd be surprised how empowering it is to have someone appreciate your good gesture when you're facing major obstacles. Sometimes the will to overcome your own struggles lies in you not complaining and still being willing to help others.

Do your best where you're at all the time.

10

A little power can make a person show their true colors. Most pretend as a matter of convenience, but once they believe they have the upper hand their abusive nature shows. Handling the gifts life gives you with grace is one of the best traits a person can have. You can't erase your abusive actions from memory, but your so-called "power" can be lost in the blink of an eye.

_____

_____

_____

_____

_____

11

Corruption lies at the core of many.
We must change our world so the people can start changing to match their surroundings. How do you tell a person surrounded by hate to love? How do you tell a person surrounded by ignorance to wise up? Information and exposure can bring about change, but are we informed? The more things change, the more they remain the same. We always address things on the surface but never dig at the roots, so the issues keeps resurfacing.

_____

_____

_____

_____

_____

12

If your heart is filled with hate, your eyes will never see the truth. Hate blinds you from seeing that you need to be better. Hate is a learned behavior that is skillfully taught by damaged individuals. A hate-filled heart is one of life's greatest opposition to positive change. Without hate, only love would exist. Would that be so bad?

_____

_____

_____

_____

_____

13

Some of us are afraid of happiness. We never truly invest the time or effort in the things that makes us happy. It's almost like an unwritten rule that investing in our personal happiness is somehow selfish, so we spend a lifetime proving we aren't selfish by sacrificing for others while neglecting ourselves.

An unbalanced life will lead to rebellion, even if it's you against your choices. Factor personal happiness into your daily decisions before you have internal revolt and external resentments.

14

Why defend your wrong deeds? An unapologetic stance is a double blow to the person already hurt by your actions. Sometimes rubbing salt in a wound is more painful that the original cut.

It's not weak to be wrong; the weakness come from refusing to accept it.

15

You never know what part of a person's past will have the most influence over their future. We all have seeds planted in us from our past experiences. Never think a person isn't knowledgeable about something without understanding where they've been. As much as we try to bury our past, it makes fingerprints all over our lives.

To thine own self be true.

_____

_____

_____

_____

_____

16

If you hang in there long enough and keep fighting,
it will eventually happen. Nothing lasts forever, so it's
impossible for all the bad to continue. Eventually, you will
get to the good. Once the good happens, remember to
cherish and enjoy it, because eventually some bad will
enter again. Life is a cycle. Never believe you'll be stuck
in one place forever; just keep pushing
until the cycle changes.

_____

_____

_____

_____

_____

17

What adjustments do others have to make to be around you? What demands does your presence require from others? Do you ever choose to see yourself as others do? Most of us are too busy living to check on how our routine actions are interpreted by those close to us. Never take how others see you for granted.

_____

_____

_____

_____

_____

18

Regardless of the good you do, bad will happen. It's life. Just deal with it, instead of wondering, "Why me?" Start thinking, "Why not me?" You are capable of handling whatever life throws at you. Just think about all the bad things that have happened that you once believed you couldn't live through. Take everything in stride, do your best and try not to burden others with your complaining, as they are handling just as much bad as you are.

_____

_____

_____

_____

_____

19

The thing about looking back is you can clearly see the mistakes you've made, but it also gives you the opportunity to see how much you've grown. It's painful to think about how wrong you were about so many things, but if you're honest enough in your assessment of your past, your bad history should never repeat itself.

I forgive myself for depending on my own understanding in my past, when it's clear to me now that I was uninformed.

_____

_____

_____

_____

_____

20

With just about everything in life, what you put in is what you get out. There's a slim minority that's fortunate enough to achieve greatness without the necessary steps, but those people aren't the ones to emulate. Fairy tales do happen, and it could happen to you if you're willing to work to make it happen. Hard work doesn't always pay off, but it puts you in the best position to win.

_____

_____

_____

_____

_____

21

It's funny how we find so many faults with our life, but others would gladly trade their lives for ours. I've sat and listen to people complain about situations, only to wonder why can't they see how blessed they are compared to others. I've always heard that every man thinks his burden is the heaviest. No one has the right to downplay what another is going through, but emotions always make things seem worse than they really are.

_____

_____

_____

_____

_____

22

Sometimes what's said in anger is truly how an individual feels. They're the thoughts they were able to suppress in their rational mind. Never let anger be your truth serum, making you say things you regretfully can't take back. Anger is no excuse to be nasty.

An apology doesn't clean its ugly residue.

23

I'm blessed to know some really good people in my lifetime. They help me keep my optimistic belief in humanity whenever I'm faced with the many evil, self-centered, cruel, hateful and judgmental people I encounter daily. Always try to focus on the good that you know, to help you move past the bad you will meet.

24

Why is it that those who go out their way to prove how much they love us are often the ones we take for granted? Why do we work so hard for approval or acceptance from those who consistently treats us poorly? The pattern is too common to be ignored.

Human nature makes us gravitate toward what we believe we are missing instead of what we already have.

_____

_____

_____

_____

_____

25

You might be willing to give, but at what cost? Giving and complaining take away from the gift. Give what you can afford so others don't have to feel guilty on the receiving end. Any gift you're not grateful to give is just for show and not a genuine gesture. A cheerful giver's gift is never contingent on the receiver's ability to reciprocate. Learn to be a selfless giver and watch your ability to give increase.

_____

_____

_____

_____

_____

26

If you don't take ownership of your situation, you can be trapped living a life that will leave you constantly disappointed. Ownership means the results are directly related to your own actions and there's no room for external blame. You will also know immediately what you need to do to fix a problem. Never live a life controlled by others and believe your life is their first priority.

27

It seems we repeat bad experiences because we haven't quite learned the lesson. In some cases, if we had truly learned the lesson we wouldn't have found ourselves in the familiar bad situation. If life is determined to make you better, stop fighting it and just be better.

Pain is no fun, especially when it's self-inflicted.

_____

_____

_____

_____

_____

28

I've found that to be happy in life, you must be 100% yourself at all times, while constantly trying to improve on who you are. The key also is surrounding yourself with people who accept you 100% for who you are, while constantly encouraging you to be better.

_____

_____

_____

_____

_____

29

Never underestimate a person, because you might not know their blessings or even what's to come. Not everyone brags about what they have. You might be surprised that those you underestimate are doing better than you could ever imagine. It's never okay to believe you're somehow better than a person just because they might not be as boastful as you.

30

Don't give up, you might just be seconds away from breaking through. If you've fought this hard for this long, you might as well keep pushing. Giving up now is such a waste of the efforts you put into preparing for what you know in your heart you deserve.

Keep focused on the rewards for your labor; it's coming.

_____

_____

_____

_____

_____

31

At the end of the day, people are people. There will be those that are just there because others are. They don't mean you any good or harm, they're just there to make up numbers. Never expect too much from a person that shows you they're just along for the ride.

Invest your efforts in the people who show up regardless: the ones who never left, especially when you needed them the most.

32

I've now learned that the greatest way to leave your mark in this life is to have the greatest positive impact you can in the lives of others. Only what you've done for others will last; the rest will die with you or be destroyed after you're gone. Change lives for the better and you will leave a lasting legacy.

33

If you constantly hang around snakes, you're either a snake charmer or a snake yourself. What is the purpose of identifying who people are, complaining about their actions and then giving them full access to your life?

You can't claim you want to change but refuse to lose those you know are against the change you desire.

_____

_____

_____

_____

_____

34

Life doesn't have to be fair, it just has to be life. There's no sense in trying to question why something happened after the fact. Sometimes we have to take the good with the bad. Instead of wondering why something happened, try to find the lesson in it.

_____

_____

_____

_____

_____

35

How can we ignore the fragility of life? We've all experienced seeing someone fully involved in living their life, only to get that unexpected call that they're no longer here. We try to rationalize it so we can continue with our own lives. Truth be told, it's so scary because we realize it could easily have been us.

Why don't we live life like we know it's short and strive to enjoy every day like its our last?

36

Life might allow you the opportunity to defend or justify your wrongs, but that doesn't make it right. Some of us only pretend, but we know when we've missed the target. Remorse is only good if we would've truly done differently if given the opportunity.

_____

_____

_____

_____

_____

37

There are those who only want to hear their own truth; they're not interested in information that requires them to change their routine. Those individuals cannot grow beyond the cage they're trapped in; ones true potential is best achieved when there's room to grow.

_____

_____

_____

_____

_____

38

Don't be afraid to chase your dreams. If you try and fail, you'll be in the same position you started from. Why are we so afraid of failure when not living your dreams is worse? Are you already in that place you're fearful of getting to? Go for it with all you've got, because you truly have nothing to lose and all to gain by trying.

39

A selfish person is often that way because those around them accept their selfishness. We can all do better in holding each other accountable for our actions. It may not change the person, but it will definitely change their access to our lives.

Stop accepting the wrongs of others in silence.

_____

_____

_____

_____

_____

40

There are those who celebrate your misfortune without reason. Some people like for others to fail so they can feel better about themselves. Stop trying to figure out why they're happy about your pain; use that as a reason to cut them out of your life and motivation to bounce back.

Don't waste your energy trying to make sense of it; just continue living and learning.

_____

_____

_____

_____

_____

41

Sometimes it's not what a loved one did that hurts; it's their refusal to acknowledge and apologize for their actions. It hurts twice as bad when someone you love doesn't respect your feelings enough to show remorse.

Forgiveness comes easier when you feel the other is sorry for what they've done.

_____

_____

_____

_____

_____

42

It's easier to be misunderstood when you don't know where you stand on issues. Know yourself enough to explain your opinions. If there is any misunderstanding, it won't between you and yourself.

Never be afraid to say what you believe, because it's the only way others can understand without assuming.

_____

_____

_____

_____

_____

43

Love teaches us valuable lessons daily; not all are pleasant. Love tests our ability to love despite hurt, pain and disappointments. If love is so powerful, shouldn't it be able heal? Don't believe love is all roses; it's also finding the ability to still love after your heart has been broken. If love is real, then it must heal. Patiently wait for it to happen and don't allow your love to become hate.

44

This life we lead may seem like a never ending journey, but that's not the case. We hustle so hard seeking material things trying to win at life's race. We rack up countless achievements. like trophies on a shelf. We chase things endlessly, only to face
death all by ourselves.

_____

_____

_____

_____

_____

45

To truly love, one must allow that love manifest in others. You must be able to be so connected that your joy comes from seeing your loved one happy. Having your love exist in another is the unselfish love we are designed to experience. Loving that person so much, that their happiness is yours also, is how love is supposed to be. If we can learn to love beyond ourself then we are on the road to true love.

46

Have respect for those who don't use their circumstances as an excuse. We are often faced with reasons to become lackadaisical, but those who find the strength to persevere are always victorious. Victory isn't only measured in material gains. It can be simply getting through the day, in spite of the obstacles.

47

If a person is willing to accept our lies, we can also tell them the truth. When will we realize that the problem lies within us, and that we also have the power to change our reality? Take nothing and no one for granted. Just because they accept us with all our faults doesn't mean that we must accept those faults; we have the ability to change, to be better to them and ourselves.

48

Its okay to be right about something that happened and not say, "I told you so." If you know what you know is it that important to rub others' faces in it. Maturity is being comfortable enough in the proven knowledge that life has taught you without having to boast to others.

_____

_____

_____

_____

_____

49

Knowledge is empowering, but it should never replace or supersede your humility. Knowledge should make you a better human being, not make you feel superior. Knowledge is the key that unlocks many doors, some leading to arrogance. Life is a journey and knowledge is fuel, so keep refueling to go the distance.

50

It's so easy to accept the good people say about us, but much harder to accept any descriptions of your faults, even if it comes from a loved one. It's easy to say that none of us are perfect, until it's time to face our own imperfections. The only way to get better is to identify and acknowledge our faults.

51

My father once told me that people will be upset with you, not because of what you did or didn't do, but because of what they believe you could have done for them and didn't. Selfishness and unrealistic expectations create one-sided realities.

_____

_____

_____

_____

_____

52

It's not just about being thankful for life, it's also making sure you're doing your best with the life you're given. Being complacent or not pursuing your purpose isn't the best way of showing appreciation for your life. If you're truly thankful for LIFE, then act like it and make it count for something.

_____

_____

_____

_____

_____

53

It's only those you love that can emotionally hurt you. Never use yourself to measure someone you love. As much as you've put into loving them, they're not you. Don't expect them to behave as you do. If loved ones hurt you, don't regret loving them; just learn how to love them from a distance.

54

You might not be famous to the world, but you always have the opportunity to be a superstar to those you love. We all can achieve greatness by being the best human being we can to those who see us daily.

Leave a legacy of love and be revered by those on the receiving end. That's real star power.

_____

_____

_____

_____

_____

55

Being prepared for bad doesn't mean you're a pessimist. Sensing a potential danger and doing nothing to prepare for it is crazy. It's easier to deal with the reality of things we've done our best to prepare for. The world is full of surprises, but some things we can see coming from miles away.

_____

_____

_____

_____

_____

56

How is it you want to make changes in life when your actions depict complacency and comfort in your current situation? The process to get to where you want to be from where you are requires you doing more than you're doing now.

Are you truly ready for what it is you want?
Do your actions match your desires?

It will only happen if you start the process.

_____

_____

_____

_____

_____

57

You must protect others from what they don't know you're capable of. Only you know the dangers that lie within.
Most can only see you from the surface, so they underestimate your potential and you allow their ignorance to keep them in the dark.

_____

_____

_____

_____

_____

58

Tragedies and pain stretches us beyond what we think possible. Pain allows us to realize that regardless of our beliefs, we always have more that we can give or endure.

The harsh realities of our true limits always dwell in the fact that we are alive and must find ways of getting past our painful heartaches, wondering all the time how much more can we really handle.

59

It's okay to be optimistic about your life, but if you don't have plans in place you'll never know if you're heading in the right direction. Know what you want out of life so you can avoid the side roads that will knock you off course.

60

Hate doesn't need a reason, it doesn't have to make sense, it is what it is: hate. Stop trying to figure out the reasons why. Focus your energy on getting past the hate with solutions that will make those who hate wonder how you're doing it. If you're not hateful, then hate should make no sense to you. Stay focused on what you know.

61

Sometimes it seems that as soon as you mention any good that's happening in your life, a floodgate of bad opens up. I'm starting to believe we must continue giving thanks for the good because the bad would have happened anyway, without us having anything to give thanks for.

Be thankful for good that comes with your bad.

_____

_____

_____

_____

_____

62

A friend once told me, "You are who you were." Good people have always shown signs of good; likewise, the bad have shown bad. People adjust because of circumstances and sometimes we ignore the signals that are sent from their essence.

Trust your instincts.

_____

_____

_____

_____

_____

63

You can fail at many tests in life and still be okay. The beauty about life is we are all works in progress. You're not defined by your failures. It's what you do with the tests you pass that elevate your humanity. Keep pushing.

64

Sometimes your downfall is designed for your protection. There are times when you're placed in positions that makes you feel pain, but in time you realize that if it wasn't for that setback, things would have been worse. Be humble, even amid adversity, because it might be your life saver. In all things give thanks.

65

Life is truly difficult at times, or so it might seem. How difficult can it really be if it doesn't kill you? Is it our perception of situations that make them seem so devastating. Anything you can walk away from with your life is a reason to celebrate, because it didn't kill you. Each moment is what you believe it to be.

Don't downplay the fact that you're still alive.

_____

_____

_____

_____

_____

66

We all have the ability to be better human beings, but it's hard work. It means honestly identifying our faults and working to correct them. We often gravitate to those who makes us feel the best about ourselves, but it's those that lovingly point out our flaws who gives us the best opportunity to be better. You can spend a lifetime never knowing yourself, only the version who people tolerate.

We can be better.

_____

_____

_____

_____

_____

67

Your breath fills your body with life. Don't waste any of it breathing energy into negativity. It's so easy to lose the ability to breathe, why not spend time appreciating every breath we are able to take?

Life is short, so if we can spend time appreciating one of its simplest sources, we will have something to build upon. Don't take your breath for granted because without it life ends. Take time to breathe through life.

_____

_____

_____

_____

_____

68

Often times it seems the truth doesn't matter. It's just the perception of what others believe that controls our reactions. If I'm broke or broken but I can create an image of wealth or stability, the truth only matters to me. People are only concerned about what others think of them instead of who they truly are. The world is filled with full-time pretenders who protect their image daily with lies.

The truth doesn't matter in a world of lies.

_____

_____

_____

_____

_____

69

I rise everyday believing with a sense of purpose that greatness is my destiny. Nothing that happens in my daily life can make me waver from the belief that I was created to be awesome. Though my current situation may not reflect this, my insides remain upbeat and focused on my bright future.

Never give up on your dreams.

_____

_____

_____

_____

_____

70

When I was younger, I prayed for wisdom, knowledge and understanding. I did not realize pain, suffering and experience were going to be the teachers. Too many times we wish for results, not thinking about the process. Be careful what you hope or pray for; make sure you are willing to endure the process to achieve them.

_____

_____

_____

_____

_____

71

There are certain lessons you can only learn by living. The good thing is that it can also come from the mistakes of others. Be attentive enough in life so that you're not guilty of what you despise in others.

Lessons are all around; it's up to you to make your life an example that others can follow. Live and learn from all mistakes, not just your own.

72

Time might heal most things, but there are some hurts that time alone will never heal. Constant reminders of unresolved hurt can lead to internal destruction. Some wounds can't just be left to time, as it only puts a thin layer over a sensitive spot.

Spend the time cleaning, dressing and attending to your emotional wounds so that with time you will heal properly.

73

You can do things with the best of intentions that can still turn out disastrous. Please remember your original intentions when you're being blamed for the end results, as chances are you're the only one that will.

Things don't always work out as planned, but one can find comfort in knowing the result wasn't the plan.

74

Panic can really throw you off your game and make the simplest of problems seem catastrophic. Panic also makes you grab at quick fixes, which normally aren't the best solutions.

If you're grounded in the understanding that anything can happen at anytime, you'll panic less when faced with a situation that is trying to appear bigger than it is.

_____

_____

_____

_____

_____

75

If you don't continue to try and do your best,
you will miss out on great moments that can make
your current situation more tolerable.
Small victories in trying times breed hope.

Never stop trying your best.

76

As hard as you try, you can never get it right all the time. You must allow room for mistakes. There is nothing wrong with allowing others to see your quest to be better by admitting your mistakes graciously.

Your ego is the only one expecting you to be perfect.

_____

_____

_____

_____

_____

77

Family is so very important, but we must make honest assessments of family members and love them for who they are and stop behaving as if they are always right because of blood. One of the hardest lessons I've learned is that you can disagree with a loved one and still love them. Our culture often dictates that once you disagree it means you don't love someone, or we are now enemies. Love must remain truthful to be real love.

_____

_____

_____

_____

_____

78

Unconditional love is when you can still feel it even when the one you love is causing you grief. It offers no resistance and requires no effort from you. Learn to love through disappointments and disagreements.
It is the best kind of love.

_____

_____

_____

_____

_____

79

It's almost impossible to live a life without hope. Through the midst of it all, we must have the belief that it will be better soon. Hope gives us the opportunity to live beyond our current situations and to get to the greatness that lies ahead.

Never lose hope in a brighter future, just keep pushing.

80

How can you not appreciate what you have when it was so very hard to achieve it? You would think the pain you went through would make you realize you're worth everything you have.

Take the time to reflect on where you've been so you LOVE and accept where you are now.

_____

_____

_____

_____

_____

81

Never feel that you know someone well enough to always predict their actions. People will only allow you to see what they want you to know. Just because you would act a certain way in a situation does not mean someone else would do the same. Don't place your personal expectations on others.

_____

_____

_____

_____

_____

82

You can't be everything to everyone else and nothing to yourself. Never spread yourself so thin trying to please others that you don't have the energy to do what is required for your happiness. Making sure you're taken care of isn't selfish, it's self love. Make sure you're part of the equation or it will never add up for you.

_____

_____

_____

_____

_____

83

Give your ALL to whatever you commit to doing so you can always be at peace with the results. You will know where you stand if failure occurs, based on your internal guilt. Others might not notice, but you know where you dropped the ball. Most times you get out what you put in.

_____

_____

_____

_____

_____

84

A friend told me that most people are scared to live naked, being stripped of all the insecurities life has clothed them with. The naked truth of who you are is often hidden behind your thoughts of what others may think about your truth. Live naked and free as you were designed to be, without worrying. Be yourself in its purest form and experience a freedom the world can never destroy.

_____

_____

_____

_____

_____

85

Family should love and accept you for who you are. Their love shouldn't be contingent on what is pleasing to them. Love is acceptance with the freedom to disagree without ridicule or malice. Love should strengthen, encourage or praise and not blame, chastise or discourage.

Love can't hate.

86

If your eulogy was written today, would you be satisfied with what was written? Find your purpose so when your chapter ends, you'll be proud of the legacy you've left and the lives you were blessed to have touched.

Live to make a positive mark in the hearts of others.

87

You must be present in your own life. Living for others is a great attribute but there must be a heavy sprinkling of your needs and desires in life for true happiness. Too often we get lost in the equation of our own life to where it never adds up. If you're not important to you, it's easy for others follow suit.

Demand more for yourself from yourself.

_____

_____

_____

_____

_____

88

If we all think a change for the better is impossible, how will it ever occur? Sometimes we adjust to mediocrity, thinking that's just how it has to be. The brave few who take a stand always end up changing the reality of those who never thought it was possible. History has proven that we don't like change and we are comfortable accepting wrong, so long as we all do it together.

_____

_____

_____

_____

_____

89

So you gave it your best, sacrificed unselfishly, and it failed. Do you now stop dreaming of being successful? No one knows your passion, desires or determination like you do. Keep believing in yourself, correct your errors and never make the fact that others failed you be your reason to quit on your dreams.

_____

_____

_____

_____

_____

90

How long are you going to let yourself be held hostage by your past? It seems that you believe everyone who is aware will judge you. Is it them or is it you? Most of us are unable to forgive ourselves for our past, so we timidly approach situations believing we are still our yesterdays. Move forward by letting go and demanding respect for who you choose to be today.

_____

_____

_____

_____

_____

91

The more you know is the more you will grow. Never be afraid to do your research. There are those banking on your ignorance, hoping you will remain comfortable in just maintaining what you know. Some of us are simply afraid of the unknown so we pretend to know it all, never breaking free from the bondage of our ignorance.

_____

_____

_____

_____

_____

92

If your happiness is so important, why are you so focused on the things that make you sad? You can clearly articulate all the problems in your life, but find difficulty expressing what brings you joy. Do you know what really makes you happy? Are those the things you focus on daily or are you caught up in the regular routine of identifying all the wrongs? Life is so short; we should put most of our energy in the pursuit of happiness.

_____

_____

_____

_____

_____

93

There are so many of us that live an unnecessary life of false pretense, never allowing ourselves or the world the opportunity to know the true us. You can never fulfill your destiny if you keep pretending. Freedom and happiness await you beyond your fears.

It's okay to be yourself, no one is perfect.

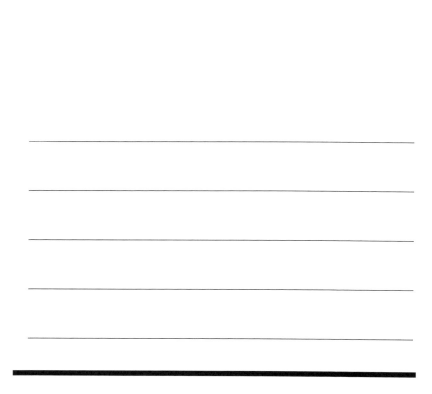

94

"It soon be done, all my troubles and trials
when I get over on the other side."

I can't help but think of all the hidden meanings that led
to passivity. It's never okay to stay dormant, waiting
for others to start making a difference. Those that act
achieve; those that don't always sit waiting and wanting.

_____

_____

_____

_____

_____

95

The "blame game" only works for those with no interest in getting better. Oftentimes the real culprit is the one most adamant about it not being their fault. Learn to accept life as a constant learning process, providing opportunities daily to get better through experiences. Mistakes can only be negative if you learned nothing from them. The rest are just lessons learned as a student of life.

_____

_____

_____

_____

_____

96

It's okay to be happy. Too often we get nervous when things are going good. Being a continuous victim of negativity, we begin to always expect the worst. Allow yourself to live in the moment of your blessing, no matter how small. Give yourself the permission to enjoy the joy that comes with recognizing how good it is to be alive.

_____

_____

_____

_____

_____

97

It's not hard to find things in life to be thankful for; the problem is not taking the time to appreciate them. The same way we take our loved ones for granted, we are guilty of overlooking our daily blessings. Gratitude is a sweet elixir that should be used daily in life to make bitter things more palatable.

98

Sometime the results of your negative actions surprise even you. The ripple effect may end up affecting the ones you care about. A negative act can take on a life of its own, creating many victims in its aftermath.

Choose wisely at moral crossroads,
your actions are not just yours.

99

You can't hide from yourself, so no one has to tell you if you're giving it your all; you know. When you've truly given it your all, there's is no guilt.

No one should outwork you at your life.

Get better at being better; it's a labor of love.

100

The bad habits we have are still choices; none of us are robots, so we can't say they happen involuntary. It's much easier to claim that's just how we were born, instead of the painful reality that it's our doing.

Life is short, if we are to get better it will require effort and not excuses.

_____

_____

_____

_____

_____

101

Sometimes it's better not to say anything if you know your words won't make the situation better. Emotionally, we know where our words come from and we can't bring our hurt to an already painful situation.

Never be selfish in your desires to feel better.

102

If you can't find something internally that makes you proud of yourself, then you might not be trying hard enough at life. You must keep yourself motivated by identifying reasons why you're uniquely awesome; it has nothing to do with arrogance. It's just keeping your belief that your life is a special gift. Know your worth.

_____

_____

_____

_____

_____

103

If we were to act on all of our thoughts, just imagine how shocked others would be. Self control is key, but don't act as if you haven't considered doing some things others have done. Be thankful for who you are, but have compassion for those who succumb to the thoughts you kept inside. We are all capable of evil, some of us are not strong enough to resist.

104

You must at some point realize how blessed you are.
You've come this far complaining about the things that
have gone wrong in your life, not realizing how much
has gone right. Nothing is wrong in aspiring to be better,
but it would help if you were grateful and appreciative
of what you already have. Are you judging your life by
what others have, or are you really looking where you're
coming from to where you are now?
Celebrate your blessings.

_____

_____

_____

_____

_____

105

If you surround yourself with positive, progressive people, you'll be optimistic even in difficult times, as someone will always encourage you. Negative people drain your energy and make bad situations worse. Choose wisely knowing you are a part of the company you keep.

_____

_____

_____

_____

_____

106

If you take the time to be a true friend to someone, letting your guards down or caring honestly, over time a bond of respect can develop. For every negative person or bad relationship you experience, the joy of the ones who love and appreciate you makes life so worthwhile.

Hope all your love seeds sowed bring you fruits.

107

Quality things always maintain their value. You have to know your worth, be it in your career, relationships or personal life. There will always be times when you have to prove your worth; never cheapen yourself by not knowing your true value. Be the standard by which all prices are set.

108

We should learn something new daily. If you don't, it's either you're not paying attention or you believe you know it all. Try to understand the things you don't know about instead of ignorantly fearing or ignoring them. Make your peace with learning, so you can do your part in teaching others. Then, we can all be better humans.

_____

_____

_____

_____

_____

109

The decisions made today would be so different if we could see tomorrow. That's why it's always best to have a check system in place, reminding you to make balanced decisions, as anything is possible. Never think it can't happen to you simply because it hasn't yet.

Faith protects, but action prepares.

_____

_____

_____

_____

_____

110

Why is so hard to wish others well and really mean it? Chances are, the effort they put into whatever success they have is the reason they are successful. Be happy for others and use them as examples of what is possible if you put effort into your dreams.

Your day will come if you put the work in.

111

Is the truth really necessary? It's difficult to live in the truth of our realities. We have difficulties handling the harsh truth, especially about ourselves. What others believe isn't necessarily the truth, but it's important to have dialogue so we can set the record straight.

The truth isn't necessarily right or wrong,
it's just the truth and must be accepted.

112

Regardless of how good you are at something, complacency can take it all away. Never get too comfortable that you stop putting the effort into being good at what you do. Keep working hard at working hard, it's what brings you the results that others admire.

_____

_____

_____

_____

_____

113

One of the greatest joys in life is having a friend that has stood the test of time, allows you to be yourself in your purest form, corrects you when you're wrong and listens to your complaints. Never underestimate their importance; just look how many battles you've faced. You couldn't have made it without them. Forget telling them; show them the love they deserve today.

114

You're failing yourself whenever you go into situations thinking others are better than you. Respecting what a person does has nothing to do with you believing you're capable of doing the same. When we start putting other humans above ourselves, we give ourselves excuses not to learn new things. With effort, education and exposure, all playing fields are level.

115

Self love doesn't mean you hate others, and confidence is different from arrogance. We don't have to be apologetic about who we are or the work we have put in to achieve success. Why do we have to be docile or passive?

Is it that most in society are not comfortable with us achieving, or the slave mentality that if we celebrate accomplishments God or the powers that be will take it away? Really wake up and check yourself.

_____

_____

_____

_____

_____

116

Try to remember that your current situation doesn't determine your life's worth. You're way more than your temporary circumstances. Just keep living and working hard to be the you that you always knew was possible. Never stop believing in your potential.

117

Finding out things in life for yourself is better than living following the masses. Most of us are so programmed we question nothing, unless we are told to by our programmers. Your every thought is uniquely yours in this information-filled universe. Exercise your freedom to not be indoctrinated; be a free thinker without fear.

Connect the dots for yourself.

118

If you see yourself in your kids, it can be such a wonderful feeling, especially when it's the good things you've passed on. Just remember, however, that kids also pay attention and mimic your bad habits, so be prepared to face yourself at its worst. Kids are true reflections of who raised them.

_____

_____

_____

_____

_____

119

Never be so predictable that others know your every move. Life is constantly changing and it's always good to evolve. However, never change the good you do, as that will always be needed.
Let others know they can depend on you.

Be consistent in your good deeds for the right reasons.

_____

_____

_____

_____

_____

120

It's possible to live your entire life never being honest with who you really are. You compromise to adjust to your surroundings all the time, losing touch with your inner self. Love is the key to free you from silly insecurities, allowing you to truly be yourself in the purest form. Learn to give and receive love without expecting perfection.

_____

_____

_____

_____

121

Most times we end up being hypocrites to ourselves in life. Our gut or spirit warn us of an impending problem with a person, but we ignore it and pretend all is well. Protect your private space by listening to your inner self and proceeding with caution.

_____

_____

_____

_____

_____

122

You could die today and the things you have done up to this point would be your legacy. Your accomplishments won't be measured against anyone but yourself and your legacy will only matter to those you have impacted. Live bold, chase your dreams, let your actions show others how much you love and care for them and you will leave a mark on this world that will last after you're gone.

_____

_____

_____

_____

_____

123

I wish there was a way I could ignore the terrible things happening in the world daily. Maybe then I wouldn't get so annoyed at those not paying attention. It so easy to get overwhelmed with all that's going on. I'm beginning to wonder if ignorance might be better.

A few always carry the load of many.

_____

_____

_____

_____

_____

124

The good that exists in you must be identified, nourished and built upon, because this cruel world can easily convince you to be evil. Evil is so prevalent today that good is becoming an anomaly. It's easier to do what is readily accepted by the masses than to stand up for what you believe is good.

Seek out those who hold you accountable to the good they know you're capable of and prove them right.

_____

_____

_____

_____

_____

125

The art of love can't be painted with words. It has to be created by actions that stain the canvas of life with permanent ink that lasts a lifetime.

A true love can't be rushed and will increase in value long after the artist is gone.

_____

_____

_____

_____

_____

126

Love is pure and simple; it's our own interpretation of what love should be that can tarnish it. Love never changes; it's our unrealistic expectations of it that end up causing us emotional issues.

Love remains the same.
Love doesn't change: only people do.

_____

_____

_____

_____

_____

127

Sometimes those we love only disappoint us because we measure their actions using our love. We can never use ourselves to judge others. The harsh reality is that you can't force someone to love you the way you love them; it's up to you to decide what you'll accept.

128

The secret desires of your heart will corrode your insides and eventually disrupt your reality if they're not properly addressed. You can never hide from yourself, so it's better to be honest about what you are feeling inside than pretending otherwise.

_____

_____

_____

_____

_____

129

How difficult is it to really be a good human being. We all know what we expect from others, but we are hesitant to give what we require. Too many of us are selfish in how we approach life. We want it all, but refuse to give our all. The world is stuck in a lopsided cycle of givers and takers.

Live a balanced life.

_____

_____

_____

_____

_____

130

Doing the right thing shouldn't be difficult. We are often worried about how our choices will affect us, instead of focusing on what's RIGHT. A very wise woman has been telling me for years to do what's right, not because of what I'll get in return. We must all learn to take our emotions out of our decision making, especially when it affects others.

_____

_____

_____

_____

_____

131

If you can't clearly define things that makes you happy, how will happiness be your reality? We don't spend enough time identifying things that make us happy and making sure they're present in our lives.

Happiness has to be important to you for it to be achieved. We spend more time trying to figure out what makes others happy instead of ourselves.

_____

_____

_____

_____

_____

132

The best version of you requires you to push past what you thought was already your best. A person who challenges you to be better than you are, isn't saying you're not good, they just know you can be GREAT. Greatness isn't perfection, it's just an understanding that you can always improve on who you are, if you keep working hard at it.

133

I've heard that you can't put clean water in a dirty container. So many claim they want to change. No matter how hard you try, the dirt inside you will contaminate the good trying to enter.

Change needs a clean vessel to start with.
Live and let live.

_____

_____

_____

_____

_____

134

Careful what you wish for in life because you might not be up for the process that comes along with it. Most times we are focused on the end results, not realizing the steps necessary to get there. Wisdom, knowledge and understanding requires you going through some stuff.

A great relationship requires hard work, and success involves so much effort that it's only attained by a few. Make sure you're willing to put in the work for the things you're wishing for.

135

It's impossible to change the mistakes from our past, but it's very important that we learn from them for the future. Carry guilt forward from life's errors is like chaining your legs to the starting blocks in a race.

No one is perfect, but lessons are easier to carry forward than the burdens of guilt. Learn how to lighten your load through self-forgiveness.

_____

_____

_____

_____

_____

136

Do things for the right reason or purpose when you're doing for others. If you give with an ulterior motive or expect something in return, it takes away from the gift.

We tend to be offended whenever we're not rewarded for something we've giving away. If it was given, then how can it still be for you. A gift is so much sweeter without strings attached from the giver.

_____

_____

_____

_____

_____

137

If the evil you silently watch occurs without any corrective actions, it will eventually affect you too. When your gut clearly identifies something as wrong and you stay silent because you think it does not affect you, your silence is you condoning the bad behavior.

Watching your neighbors' house burn down without sounding an alarm is like striking the first spark yourself. Evil gains strength when it's allowed to flourish without resistance.

138

It's impossible for everyone to like you or always say good things about you, so just get over yourself and don't breathe life into negativity. Live life above pettiness so that whenever they rise up, folks will ignore them and pity them. Live so others can't define you; only your actions will. It's not what you are called, but what you answer to. Know yourself for yourself.

139

A great feeling is not just having a person you call upon when bad happens, it's having someone you can't wait to share good news with. Often times we are reluctant to share the good, but having someone you know will celebrate your joys is one of life's treasures.

Pay close attention and appreciate those who are happy about your happiness.

_____

_____

_____

_____

_____

140

It's better to identify your faults; accept them so you can genuinely change for the better. Living in denial, pretending they don't exist or blaming others for your actions will keep you stuck in your failures.

If you really want to get better, you must first know that you need to be better.

141

Growing older can be scary if you believe you haven't accomplished your dreams so far in life. However, if you've sown seeds into the development of others or played any positive role in a younger person's life, you will feel a sense of accomplishment as your years extend. Find reasons outside yourself to celebrate milestones in life.

_____

_____

_____

_____

_____

142

For you to really move forward, you must forgive yourself for what you've done to remain stuck. Asking for forgiveness from others or forgiving others is great, but true freedom comes with learning how to forgive yourself and letting your guilt go.

_____

_____

_____

_____

143

Every time we don't stand up for what we know to be right, a piece of our self worth dies. We can't be fearful of repercussion to the point that we force ourselves to live with internal turmoil. Being quiet or lying to yourself on the outside causes an internal decay that will manifest itself by destroying your self confidence.

Free yourself from the guilt of not being yourself.

144

You can blame others all you want, but the consequences of your actions will always be yours to live with. Blaming others keeps you in a revolving cycle of making mistakes.

_____

_____

_____

_____

_____

145

Never let your anger or current life situations make you be mean to those you interact with daily. Everybody is dealing with something you may not be able to see on the surface.

We can't all match fire with fire. Try to be the reason a person's day is better as opposed to being a continuation of what's wrong.

_____

_____

_____

_____

_____

146

True loving isn't easy. Truly loving a person through their imperfections, failures, drama, ignorance, anger and arrogance is a special gift. If you know you have someone with enough patience to love you in spite of your shortcomings, why not take the time to shower them with appreciation?

Balance all you put them through by amplifying the reasons they fell in love with you in the first place. Work on making your good outweigh your bad. Show love.

_____

_____

_____

_____

_____

147

Sometimes we allow others to not only control our happiness, but we also use them as validation for our success. Be secure in yourself so others can only join the party in progress.

Your happiness shouldn't wait on others.

148

Life is simple, just be honest in our daily decisions and deal with the consequences. Approach each situation with love and patience, never forgetting our humanity. If life was really that simple, everyone would do it. However, life is a constant struggle. We all know what to do but get amnesia once certain pressures are applied. We are all works in progress, aspiring to be better in whatever we believe to be important. Let's try at least to shift our focus to happiness and start there.

149

What's wrong with being happy about another's success while working hard and patiently waiting on yours to happen? Another person's success doesn't equal your failure, especially if you played a positive role in their process. Negative thinking breeds hate, but clean thoughts open the doors of love and opportunity.

_____

_____

_____

_____

_____

150

As we get older, it becomes clearer that life is short. We don't have the luxury of wasting precious moments being unhappy. We should spend moments living our truth. Happiness must be a choice, because unhappiness is by our choosing. This life may be short, but there is so much we can do if we choose to live it to its fullest.

_____

_____

_____

_____

_____

151

The big picture is often times made a finished product by people you never see at the celebrations. The unsung heroes are always behind the scenes, sacrificing so others can enjoy the fruits of their labor. Have respect for those who do things for the love, pride or principles without seeking recognition or praise.

_____

_____

_____

_____

_____

152

Doing what everyone else does is easy; putting in the work to be different is challenging. You must understand that those who go with the flow will always take notice of those that choose a different direction. No one likes to be reminded that they're followers, especially if they're not happy with the results. You chose the road, so you must accept what comes with it.

_____

_____

_____

_____

_____

153

Being mentally or emotionally tired seems to be more frequent now than being physically tired. We now wake up feeling drained. The pressures of the lives we choose to live can be overbearing without balance. We must set aside time for ourselves before we become a slave to the rat race. Fight for balance.

_____

_____

_____

_____

_____

154

How are we supposed to effectively bring about any real change when we can't come together on the simplest of things that affect us all?

_____

_____

_____

_____

_____

155

Life has to be more than just surviving struggles or adversities. At what point do we understand that life is to be enjoyed? If all we're doing is surviving, all we're doing is existing. Life provides abundance, so there is always room to enjoy the process.

_____

_____

_____

_____

_____

156

Sometimes it's hard to chase your dreams in a world filled with dream killers and non-dreamers. Your dreams have to be bigger to you than all the negativity you'll encounter while in pursuit of them. You must remember that your dreams are yours and can't be affected by others unless you allow it.

Keep chasing your dreams until they're your reality.

_____

_____

_____

_____

_____

157

I don't believe men were taught how to love properly. For generations we were force-fed a chauvinistic view of how love is supposed to be. Love isn't a sign of weakness, nor should it ever be a power struggle. Love is supposed to be free and vulnerable. One should love without the fear of being hurt. If if hurt comes, it's not love that was wrong; it was who you chose to love.

Love is the greatest gift life has to offer.

_____

_____

_____

_____

_____

158

Being right is relative, because most times it means someone else was wrong. Being right is normally just a perception based on what you believe to be true, but your truth may not match up with the reality of others.

Understand that "right" shouldn't make you self-righteous.

159

It's very simple find your purpose. Prioritize your life with what's important. Find love from within and you'll never be without. Speak as if your words are smiling. Let life unfold while you do your best. Always maintain a balanced life and keep a spiritual connection. If it doesn't sound simple, it's because you don't realize
it's simply up to you.

_____

_____

_____

_____

_____

160

Each day should bring you one step closer to being a better human, or at the very least better able to cope with struggles. What is the sense in surviving the hardships of yesterday if you didn't learn anything?

Life is all about growing from our experiences; learn from what you've lived.

161

If you only surround yourself with those scared of hurting your feelings, you'll never fully grow as a person. If you can't see yourself as a work in progress, others won't be comfortable in helping you become better. Love those with enough patience to stick with you through your learning processes of life.

162

Do laws define lawlessness? Does religion define sin?
Does governance define rebellion? Do we really create
our own realities? Since knowledge makes us aware of
ignorance, then it makes sense that a person is a fool to
what they don't know. Is not knowing really foolish,
or protection from an unwanted reality?

_____

_____

_____

_____

_____

163

Sometimes we are scared to do what would make us happy, because we are worried about what others might think. Bravery is knowing the possible dangers but still going ahead, with hopes of victory.

Happiness is a victory that's worth the risk.

164

Make your life be the difference in all the lives you touch.
Your life legacy can be the one that changes the future
of those that it touched. Take your purpose seriously
enough to leave your world better than you entered it.

_____

_____

_____

_____

_____

165

If you knew where some of us have been or the things we've been through, you would celebrate our blessings instead of being jealous. What may look like success to you may be nothing more than preservation or survival to others. Learn to appreciate the good in others, because it takes nothing away from you.

166

What I've learned from Usain Bolt is that if we allow people to be comfortable in who they are, they can achieve greatness. Never try to change the essence of a person; true comfort breeds confidence and strength in one's ability to succeed. Encourage people to be true to who they are and accept them with love.

_____

_____

_____

_____

_____

167

At some point we must evaluate if a person brings more good than bad to our lives and adjust accordingly. Too often we allow people to take up undeserving residence in our personal space at a sacrificial cost only to us. Value your personal space enough to only allow a balanced environment. Fill your space with those who give more than they take.

_____

_____

_____

_____

_____

168

Risk takers and dreamers shape and change the world. Some of us can't ignore the desire to explore beyond our current situation, regardless of the obvious obstacles. Failure is no match for the passion that burns inside of a dreamer. Dream big, but do the work necessary to change your circumstances and then the world.

_____

_____

_____

_____

_____

169

If you purposely do things knowing it will make it harder for others that come after you, you're a selfish individual. Too many times we are only concerned about ourselves, not seeing how our actions adversely affect our fellow humans. Be mindful of your steps in life; make sure you're not just stepping on others to succeed.

170

Those that truly love you and are always there shouldn't be taken for granted. We often forget the ones most loyal to us because they require nothing from us. We spend most of our time trying to please those we believe we have to impress. We step outside of ourselves to try and gain acceptance, while ignoring those who have always accepted us at our core.

Love those who love you, as they deserve the most.

_____

_____

_____

_____

_____

171

I'm at an uncomfortable level of consciousness where I'm starting to question the things I've been taught. Have patience with me while I try to decipher the things that are weighing heavily on my mind. There is too much that doesn't add up, but my indoctrinated mind refuses to let go. If the truth is the light, then how is it possible for so many to be in the dark?

_____

_____

_____

_____

_____

172

Everyone should at least feel like a celebrity to their families or close friends. You should feel like you're important. Your presence should be appreciated, your words should matter and you should be given accolades for your bodies of work. If we celebrated those close to us, we might end up with more happy people than some of the emotionally broken vessels we deal with daily.

_____

_____

_____

_____

_____

173

I've often heard it said that evil people always seems to get ahead in life. Is it that they succeed because they're evil, or should their success be attributed to the fact that they will do whatever is necessary to get it done? We often times misinterpret end results based upon our perception of right or wrong.

In the end, it's always actions that brings results.

_____

_____

_____

_____

_____

174

To live without a dream is to live just waiting to die. For the short time that we are here on earth, we must strive to accomplish all we can to the best of our abilities. What is the purpose of taking all your gifts and potential back with you, when you were given them to be successful in this life?

Dare to dream big and spend your life making them your reality.

_____

_____

_____

_____

_____

175

How close are you to achieving your dreams? Are you still optimistic about reaching your inner expectations in this lifetime? How far along are you in your plans for success? Life is getting shorter, and at some point you must go for it. Settling for less than your dreams is a reality for most; not because the dreams were impossible, but because most of us never really gave ourselves a chance.

You were born for more than to just exist.

176

No matter how much good happens in your life, if your mind stays focused on what's wrong, you will never be happy. Although you might have major problems, good things happen daily. Life is harder if we only focus on trials instead of victories and sadness instead of joy.

_____

_____

_____

_____

_____

177

It's funny how we can go through some hardships in life, get past them realizing how blessed we are, then panic immediately when faced with the next challenge. Each hurdle jumped should give
us confidence for the next hurdle.

We should never forget our past blessings
or the strength within.

_____

_____

_____

_____

_____

178

Why do we believe we have the ability to change a person's bad habits? We are given several examples of bad, but we believe our good will somehow penetrate the bad to produce good. It's okay to expect good from a person when bad is consistent. However, it's time to protect yourself. See people for who they are and hold them accountable for their actions.

_____

_____

_____

_____

_____

179

Often times as humans we are worse than the people we cast judgment on daily. We are all humans, so we are capable of all things; the only thing that separates us is our choices. The ability to choose comes from life experience and not necessarily a position of greatness.

You're no better than those you choose to chastise; a very thin line separates us one from another.

_____

_____

_____

_____

_____

180

Love needs honesty to reach its full potential; it can't exist within lies or deception. Love me enough to tell me truth and allow me the opportunity to deal with the realities of its impact.

You're not helping me to grow by lying to me, all you're doing is choosing what you believe is the easiest way out. Love can survive the truth, but it's damaged by lies.

_____

_____

_____

_____

_____

181

If you lose yourself in the midst of your struggle, your struggles will become your reality. Holding on to who you are will allow hope to shine through. Never lose faith in yourself or your ability to rebuild. Without faith, you have no future. Stay prepared and focused.

182

This world can be such a cold place, sometimes it makes it easy to look the other way and not extend yourself to others. An opportunity to do an unselfish act can be so empowering. In the stillness of your thoughts, you know you chose not to help and your conscience will remind you.

Stay true to your soul.

_____

_____

_____

_____

_____

183

It's difficult for me to believe that as humans we are not spiritual beings. I'm not talking religion; we sometimes connect with others on a level that's beyond words. The energy of good can be felt, and so can the presence of negativity. I believe we have stepped away from our spirituality because of lack of knowledge, and by default lost a major part of our humanity. Without spirituality, there is too much of our essence that can't be explained. I am a spiritual being connected to the numerous energies that exist in the universe.

I love the spirit that moves within us all.

184

One of the main reasons we have mean, obnoxious individuals is because their so-called "loved ones" enable and tolerate them. No one's behavior is etched in stone; they're normally surrounded by people who take it for granted. The rest of the world has to suffer for it.

_____

_____

_____

_____

_____

185

There are so many amongst us that choose to live a life of unhappiness. Too many pretend perfection, not realizing that true happiness can be found in their truth.

Find the core source of your happiness
and build your life around that.

_____

_____

_____

_____

_____

186

If you look close enough, you will see that life is a series of repeat patterns and you can often tell where something is heading. As humans, optimism always makes us feel this time will be different. Optimism is a good thing when coupled with a sense of reality. You shouldn't rule out your past experiences.
History often repeats itself.

_____

_____

_____

_____

_____

187

There is a HUGE difference between arrogance and confidence. It's impossible to be humble and arrogant at the same time, but a confident person can still remain humble. Never be so into your accomplishments that you think you're above others.

_____

_____

_____

_____

_____

188

Hurt shouldn't breed hurt, and pain shouldn't want to see pain. We often times forget the struggles we deal with when we can prevent another from going through a similar struggle. The world would be much simpler if we understood that we don't have let others suffer just because we did. It's okay to build upon love.

_____

_____

_____

_____

_____

189

If you're not passionate about something in life, you might just be existing. Passion is a force that drives you to continue doing your best. Passion is like the sun being trapped inside, exploding its rays outwards. Find your passion, grab hold and be ready to live or die for it.

190

Those who really love you will want you to succeed, but don't be surprised if that number is lower than you expected. If success were easy, the rest of the world wouldn't be so miserable. Fight hard to break free from the misery of others. You are that one in a million.

_____

_____

_____

_____

_____

191

Now is the time to set long term goals and plans for your future. Time is always moving at such a fast pace and those goals will be reality in no time.
Life can easily become a blur if you let it.

Use the time you have here to your advantage.
Don't let it slip away.

_____

_____

_____

_____

_____

192

As good or bad as things might be, one action can change your life instantly. As humans, we're normally one decision away from a change, so we can't take anything for granted. I've had the rug pulled from under me as often as I've found a rock in sinking sand. I've learned to be aware of my surroundings, as there is always a life-changing event lurking in the shadows.

_____

_____

_____

_____

_____

193

If we all live in the same world, how can we see things so differently? Our eyes seem to focus mainly on what we believe instead of what we're actually viewing. Most of the world lives in a reality created through their interpretation of facts rather than the actual facts. Nothing is really black or white; instead we all choose to exist in a gray area, and never truly accept things for what they are.

We're trying to avoid the painful truth.

_____

_____

_____

_____

_____

194

As much as you could be one problem away from everything falling apart, you could one solution or blessing away from things getting better. Constantly searching for solutions, however, makes the blows that should knock you out just another step toward victory.

_____

_____

_____

_____

_____

195

Why are we so good at complaining about what a person does wrong, but it's so hard to give them credit for their good deeds? Is it that we programmed only to discuss what's wrong and ignore what's right?

Start learning to verbally appreciate the good in others and make the world a better place.

_____

_____

_____

_____

_____

196

The true essence of what makes you happy can't be hidden behind false pretense. No matter how you try to bury it, the truth will demolish a house of lies.

_____

_____

_____

_____

_____

197

Yesterday was a difficult day for you, and that's understandable. Always believe that once you survived yesterday, today is going to be a cakewalk. Just make it through today, because tomorrow will be better. No time to dwell on the past while you're still alive.

198

Why are we so good at giving sound advice to others, but can't seem to get our own lives in order? Are we better at seeing others' mistakes, but blind to the errors of our own ways? Or, is that talking requires less effort than the actions needed for correction?

199

No one can save you from your own ignorance. If you don't take the time to examine where you stand, you won't realize you're on sinking sand until it's too late.

Never just step because you have legs; have a direction and check your foundation.

_____

_____

_____

_____

200

Lying damages the structural foundation of your character. Lies may not initially seem like a big deal until you're trying to pick up the pieces of your destroyed credibility. The truth might not be easy to handle, but at least it gives you a solid base to build upon.
Stay in your truth.

_____

_____

_____

_____

_____

201

Our mistakes will be amplified and broadcasted so much quicker than our good deeds. The key is to make our good so great that it will overshadow the bad they'll talk about. Even in an envious way, greatness is recognized.

_____

_____

_____

_____

_____

202

The blame game is so easy, everyone can play. But after the blame is placed, now what? Doesn't moving forward depend on you and your actions? The more time you focus on what you have to do, the faster you move ahead.

_____

_____

_____

_____

_____

203

Is it bad to feel as if your life isn't where it's supposed to be? Isn't it better to think it's not only where life is supposed to be, it's where you are allowed it to be? Life is nothing more than the choices we make daily, and your life is a direct result of the decisions you made. Make the necessary adjustments now before a life becomes lost.

204

It's impossible for us to all see things the same way. We must learn to see where the other person is coming from. As passionate as we may feel about a particular issue, through patience we can learn, teach and grow.

However, if conversations aren't rational or based in fact, you're wasting valuable time, so you must respectfully move on. Never be a know-it-all, but know enough to recognize when you're beating a dead horse.

_____

_____

_____

_____

_____

205

The rewards from perseverance can only be reaped by those who persevere. If we knew some of the blessings that await us, we would smile at our current struggles.

Fight to get to your rewards.

_____

_____

_____

_____

_____

206

When someone who has been consistently good to you deals you a devastating blow, it's tough to assess. You can't throw away all their good because of their error, but it's difficult to get past the hurt. Try to remember them being there for you as decide how to move forward.

Some things you can't forget, but based
on your history you must forgive.

207

After all you have been through in your life, why is it so hard to be compassionate towards others? Things you've done in the name of survival should make you conscious of others' struggles. Never be so focused on yourself that you forget we are all in this thing called life together.

Our struggles make us human.

_____

_____

_____

_____

_____

208

There are some struggles no one can help you with, regardless of how much they love you. Your personal growth requires you to go through some defining periods. Stop looking to external sources and start embracing the hard, necessary steps to be better.

Not everything requires a group effort; you become more valuable when the best version of you emerges.

_____

_____

_____

_____

_____

209

You can't tell me you're alive and healthy enough that things can't still change for the better. Really? So your temporary set back is permanent? So why didn't you die? Every ounce of life in you is reserved for you to fight for your blessings.

210

Why is it okay to bend the rules when it's in your favor and not for others? We react to things based on how they affect us. Wrong is wrong, regardless of if it is beneficial to you. Never complain about something you would have normally ignored once it was in your favor.

Don't have selective amnesia.

_____

_____

_____

_____

_____

211

Start demanding the love and respect you know you deserve instead of making excuses for why you're not getting it. Accepting less than you're worth isn't a bargain, it's just a bad deal. In love get value for value, a fair exchange is no robbery and never just give away your profits.

212

Sometimes when you're too stubborn in life, only catastrophic events can get your attention. Don't complain about how harsh your lessons are when you're the one always missing the much softer warning signs.

213

If you know what's right but don't do it, you are worse than the person who doesn't know what's right. At least they have an excuse. You gain knowledge or experience for a purpose. It's not a trophy; it's to be used for the benefit of others.
Share what you've learned by doing what's right.

_____

_____

_____

_____

_____

214

If the things you used to do routinely are now beginning to be a struggle, you should be concerned. When your joy starts slipping away, please talk about it. Depression creeps in slowly, but it can quickly take over your life. We don't talk about it enough, but the pressures of life can become unbearable for so many of us. Recognize it in yourself and lovingly identify it in others so we all can begin to enjoy the sunrise again. Depression is real.

_____

_____

_____

_____

_____

215

Hitting the panic button every time a problem occurs sets us back further each time. The best decisions are made when we remember that we've been here before and survived. Lessons learned are what we should use to prevent panic. Life always has issues. There is always a solution that requires us to be present, not panicked.

_____

_____

_____

_____

_____

216

Be a person that adds value to your loved ones lives, instead of being a constant reminder of their faults.

Prove you're a blessing to their life.

_____

_____

_____

_____

217

Sometimes it's better not to say anything if you know your words won't make the situation better. Emotionally we know where our words come from, and we can't bring our hurt to an already painful situation.

Never be selfish in your desire to feel better.

_____

_____

_____

_____

_____

218

Some of our suffering is self-inflicted based upon bad decisions. We can't always blame life for our hardships. Ownership of our struggles don't make them easier, but it does give us the ability to move on without self-pity. Own your issues, knowing you have the ability to correct them.

_____

_____

_____

_____

_____

219

Don't live with survivor's remorse. When someone you love does something wrong and are now suffering the harsh consequences, don't feel guilty. We must all be held accountable for our actions. Never feel responsible for the lessons others must learn; just continue to try and help them avoid the initial mistake.

_____

_____

_____

_____

_____

220

What will it take for you to truly understand that a change is needed? Is it not possible to learn from others mistakes? Do we really need to feel pain to understand?

The world is filled with painful examples we ignore because it hasn't happened to us yet.

_____

_____

_____

_____

221

Why is it so hard to put value on your happiness? Compromises are good to prove you're a compassionate human, but at what cost? Love, work, relationships, religion and so much more are all connected to your happiness.

Make decisions that leads to happiness instead of the continued patterns of compromises that always leave you lacking.

_____

_____

_____

_____

_____

222

Even when you're right, you can end up doing the wrong thing. If you lose focus of the big picture, your actions that are fueled by hurt, anger or disappointment can end up wrong.

Think about what you're doing and make sure it doesn't make things worse.

_____

_____

_____

_____

_____

223

Confusion is the constant state that most of us live our lives in. Most are afraid to talk about it, not realizing that everyone is just as confused as you are. Sometimes it's the best pretender that wins the prize; truth is only what is accepted by the masses.

224

Life is a trip. The bills come before the money, there are never enough hours in the day, the kids are a handful and it seems like all you do is work. Enjoy it all, because without life there would be nothing to complain about.

Just be thankful.

_____

_____

_____

_____

_____

225

I rise everyday believing that greatness is my destiny. Nothing that happens daily makes me waver from the belief that I was created to be awesome. Although my current situation may not reflect it, all my inside remains upbeat and focused on my bright future.

Never give up on your dreams.

_____

_____

_____

_____

_____

226

A difficult thing is having so much love for a person who doesn't understand the essence of who you are. Life shouldn't be about proving who you are to others, it should be about being comfortable in who you are, regardless of what others might think. It's hard because we all want others to see the best in us, but we are often judged by the worst in them. Love shouldn't be complicated; it should be honest. But honesty doesn't always mean agreeing, and isn't that still love?

_____

_____

_____

_____

227

Some people get it. They live each day to the fullest, don't sweat the small stuff, are honest to themselves and put themselves first. Then there is the rest of the unhappy world. Happiness remains a choice.

228

I've lived through some serious tragedies, but life has never stopped because of them. I quickly realize that life never stops, so neither can I.

Whatever happens, I have to keep moving.

_____

_____

_____

_____

_____

229

There is nothing more important in this world than love. Love affords us the opportunity to impact lives in ways only love can. Love is the necessary ingredient for all that is good. Start by loving yourself, then try to transfer that love to those you encounter daily.

Love should live within you and flow like a river, soaking everyone who comes in contact with it.

_____

_____

_____

_____

_____

230

I may not have all the answers, but I'm not afraid to ask the questions. Education in anything comes when we make ourselves available to learn with a curious mindset. Never live life with a closed mind void of questions; your reaction to what you learn is still your choice.

_____

_____

_____

_____

_____

231

It's hard to be who you say you are when you've never taken the time to figure out who that is. What do you really stand for in life? Is your purpose clear to others? What is your mark amongst the living? Does your life even make a difference? Only you know the truth.

_____

_____

_____

_____

_____

232

Encouragement is wonderful when you're standing on a question mark, but when you're focused, encouragement is like a rocket. Never downplay the importance of offering someone positive reinforcement during their daily struggles. We all need to know our life matters and that we are appreciated for who we are. Spread the love.

_____

_____

_____

_____

_____

233

You must have the real hard conversations with yourself to come up with conclusions you can move forward with. It's all in front of your eyes, but harsh realities prevent us from believing. Check out what's real.

_____

_____

_____

_____

_____

234

The truth may be offensive, but it's not a sin. Only those you care deeply about have the ability to hurt you deeply. It's okay to love honestly, understanding that those you love still have the ability to hurt you. It's not that loving is wrong; the wrong still lies with the corrupted individuals.

_____

_____

_____

_____

_____

235

Regardless of how good you might be on your own, you can't do it all by yourself. The help you receive from others can be an important asset to your success.

Don't be ashamed of asking for help when you need it.

_____

_____

_____

_____

_____

236

Never lose hope that things will get better. Even when your eyes can't see it, just keep believing in your heart it's possible. The key, however, is doing your best everyday, while looking for opportunities.

It's not just hope and faith; it's also surviving.

237

You can enter into certain situations with the purest intentions and there will still be a person that will judge you wrongfully. No one but you lives inside your head so stop trying to prove them wrong and work more on proving yourself right.

238

There are so many of us who know what would make us happy but are too busy living the opposite. We use life as an excuse not to live our dreams. If you can clearly define what you would be doing if you had a choice, why do you not see that the choice is yours?

You really have one life to create happiness;
don't be afraid.

239

When there are bad roads you've traveled that are familiar to you, you feel a sense of comfort as you know where they lead. This is not a good thing all the time, because you must have gone backwards at some point to be on the familiar road again. Blaze a trail while leaving proper warning signs for those behind. Keep moving forward, only going back to show others the way to success.

240

It's very important that we constantly find things to be thankful for. The tougher the times get, the more thankful we have to be about the smaller things in life. Make the adjustments to maintain hope and joy. Even if we can't give thanks for a raise or bonus, we can still be thankful for having a job. Remain thankful.

_____

_____

_____

_____

_____

241

You should be the biggest celebrity on the stage of your life, giving your all in every life performance. You must understand the direction of your director and know that each new role is an opportunity to show your world audience your versatility. In life, be that star that everyone enjoys. There is only one you, so act like you know it.

_____

_____

_____

_____

_____

242

Sometimes we passively go through life accepting everything because we lack the effort needed to achieve our goals. Don't blame life for your failures if you're just an inactive spectator in your own life.

Only you can change your direction.

_____

_____

_____

_____

_____

243

There are certain things in life you have to do daily and often. The same way you have to brush your teeth or they will decay, other areas of your life need routine attention.

Find the decaying areas in your life and tend to them.

_____

_____

_____

_____

_____

244

In life, once you embark on a mission to try and make a difference, you will become a target. It's better to wage a war for what's right than to sit on the sidelines in fear and ignorance. When the opposition arises, you know you have the enemy's attention. Your victory is your enemies fear, as they already know that it's possible. Keep fighting for the cause; your efforts will bring rewards.

_____

_____

_____

_____

_____

245

Some days, if we pay close attention, we can sense the energy and direction of our day. We must learn to pay attention to the energy that surrounds us, as they're layered with warning signs that can prevent mishaps. Listen to your inner self today and proceed accordingly.

All days are meaningful.

_____

_____

_____

_____

_____

246

An arrogant person is often force-fed their arrogance, while a humble person graciously accepts the rewards of their humility. An arrogant person will act like they are bigger than you, but a wise person knows to check their ego. Be humble, as it will soften the harsh blows of life.

_____

_____

_____

_____

_____

247

You'd be naive to think that your family and friends only speak good about you behind your back. If you could be a fly on the wall, you would hear some honesty about yourself that you wouldn't believe. The question is, why can't they tell you the truth to your face? Is it that they're hypocrites or they know your fragile ego can't handle the truth? None of us are perfect, but we must leave room for others to feel comfortable correcting us.

248

Everything happens for a reason. Your daily interactions with people during the course of the day have a lingering effect. That simply means each day you have a chance to mean something or have a positive affect in someone's life.

Make each encounter count.

_____

_____

_____

_____

249

Never be too busy that you forget to show love to the important people in your life. Don't wait until their funeral to celebrate life. Show up before it's too late.

_____

_____

_____

_____

_____

250

Until you truly find yourself, you will remain lost and confused in the world. Self-love is realizing your faults and accepting them. Finding yourself requires facing the truth of who you really are and embracing it.

Life is so much better living in your truth.

_____

_____

_____

_____

251

Someone you really trusted might cause you pain, but in the middle of that pain can lie the lesson you needed to become better. This doesn't mean that person was right for hurting you, it just means you can forgive and appreciate them for their role in
your personal development.

_____

_____

_____

_____

_____

252

When you say you're doing something from your heart, make sure your heart is in the right place. When we have a conviction of our spirit, make sure we're not championing our own stubborn beliefs. Don't act solely on your emotions without actually checking your reasons.

Feeling strongly doesn't mean you're right.

_____

_____

_____

_____

_____

253

We all like our egos stroked. Are we truly worthy of the praise, or are our loved ones just appeasing us by saying the things they think we need to hear? We must put the work in to be worthy of accolades. Never have such a fragile ego that others have to blow smoke at you for you to feel good about yourself. Let your work speak for itself and the rest will fall into place.

_____

_____

_____

_____

_____

254

Bullies normally pick on those they believe offer the least resistance to their cowardly actions. Being too passive allows weak-minded predators to believe you're prey. Never be so afraid that you become a victim of a person too blind to see how pathetic they are. Take away a bully's strength by not appearing weak; they will never try to pick a fair fight.

.

_____

_____

_____

_____

_____

255

There is nothing wrong in talking about your good habits, even if it's just to yourself. Praise isn't routinely given in society, sometimes we just need to acknowledge ourselves for the things we do right because the world can't wait to balance you by amplifying your wrongs.

Celebrate your strengths so you can find the strength to continue surviving in the world, at least do it for yourself in case others may miss your efforts.

_____

_____

_____

_____

_____

256

None of us are perfect, we ALL can work on being better human beings, we lose a little of our humanity everyday as the world gets harder. Catch yourself before you slip further into being as cold as the world we live in.

_____

_____

_____

_____

_____

257

Life is so much sweeter when you feel that your life makes a difference to someone else. When through love a loved one makes you feel loved by returning your love, life is wonderful. Love breeds love so only those who give love know how good it feels to be loved.

_____

_____

_____

_____

_____

258

Care enough to truly try make a difference in the life of someone you love without expecting something in return. Seeing others happy does not take away from your happiness. Happiness is a shared privilege we can all enjoy.

259

When you live life as a "worrier" it never stops, the mind is so powerful it keeps throwing new things at you to worry about. Instead of being a worrier, try living life as a WARRIOR. Understand that you are prepared for whatever challenges you are faced with. Give it your all.

260

Our truth helps others way more than our ability to pretend we are okay. We put pressure on each other as a society by painting the picture that we are without struggle. You never know who you may help by being honest about you are going through.

Love yourself through your imperfections.

_____

_____

_____

_____

_____

261

We must become better decision makers when it comes to our own lives, after all, life is all about choices. If we have to live with the consequences of our decisions then shouldn't good decisions be paramount? We can't always get it right but we must at least put the right amount of time and effort into the process of our choices.

262

Money is a necessary tool for survival but it shouldn't be the decision-maker in your life. Some of your most meaningful experiences might not include you profiting monetarily from them. Money doesn't equal love. Try not to love money more than the life you were predestined to live and enjoy.

_____

_____

_____

_____

_____

263

You are your biggest asset. Apply yourself in all things and you will realize your full potential. You're the constant in all of your success or failures so start believing that once you're in the mix, the outcome will be great.

Believe in yourself.

_____

_____

_____

_____

_____

264

Lessons are wasted when all we focus on is what we have been through, try to think instead of all the things you'll able to accomplish with your new found experience. Life is for living. Never dwell on your setbacks. Learn from them and turn that into new energy and motivation.

_____

_____

_____

_____

_____

265

Love isn't a game. Every situation where love is involved should strengthen your soul. The heart is fragile, love should be respected and protected. If you choose to play games with love, then love becomes the loser.

Protect and respect your love.

_____

_____

_____

_____

_____

266

It is said that we are all created equal. If there are some of us that achieve greatness, then why not you? Use the examples of others to know it's possible for you as well. Instead of being jealous, get motivated knowing you are equipped and also capable of greatness.

It may be tough but you can do it, start with changing your mindset.

_____

_____

_____

_____

_____

267

It's interesting how we find so many faults with our life but others would gladly trade their lives for ours. I've always wondered why we can't see how blessed we are. There's a saying that goes "who feels it knows it". Every man think his burden is the heaviest. No one has the right to downplay what another is going through but emotions always make things seem worse than they really are.

_____

_____

_____

_____

_____

268

Love is always the answer even when it's easier said than done. We must practice what we preach until it is a reality. Sometimes others action makes it difficult for love to manifest, but you must still do your part in the process.

_____

_____

_____

_____

_____

269

We are all connected. Your life is going to influence others whether you realize it or not. Once you understand and take ownership of this fact, you will try to be a good influence to others. Selfishly trying to separate yourself and thinking that you're just living for you, will only create more selfish people.

Live as if you know someone you love is watching.

_____

_____

_____

_____

_____

270

It's interesting how we are only able to see what's on the surface of everyone's existence. Imagine if we were able to see all the hurt, disappointments, insecurities that we all carry inside daily. Think about how often we inadvertently drive a nail into an already existing wound.

We must always consider the possibilities that just like us, others are fighting a battle they may not be open about. Don't abuse others with irresponsible actions, as you also have things you're protecting.

_____

_____

_____

_____

_____

271

Do you ever wonder if you are LIVING up to your true potential? Is this all you were born to do? Are you satisfied the way life turned out? The bottom line is we were all designed with specific greatness within us. We get to various levels in life, become complacent, forgetting that there's so much more in us.

Never limit yourself to your present situation, keep rising towards your greatest potential.

272

Understand that you can't control the actions of others. What you can do is control your expectations. All humans are capable of good and bad. Knowing our capabilities should make us more tolerant of each others actions. Expect good always but know bad is also a possibility. Unrealistic expectations lead to disappointments.

273

Love is an important word but until you meet someone who actually brings meaning to the word, it will remain a mystery. The act of love requires letting go of all your insecurities, free falling into the safety net of true acceptance. If you're still pretending around a loved one then you haven't mastered the art of true love. The key is that person who uses their love as an equalizer to your faults and makes you want to be a better person.

_____

_____

_____

_____

_____

274

If misery loves company, why can't happiness love happiness? Shouldn't success be happy for success? Are we programmed just for the negative or does the opposite also apply? I want to focus my energies on the positives so that I can become better. I am welcoming all the good that surrounds me, while trying to match it with the good that exists within me.

Let's all meet up somewhere together in love.

_____

_____

_____

_____

_____

275

If you understood the significant role you play in your happiness, you wouldn't waste time focusing on negative people trying to hold you back. Use the gifts you have been given to achieve happiness. If you don't truly believe you should be happy you will never fight for it.

_____

_____

_____

_____

_____

276

There has to be room in all relationships for disagreements. No one is perfect, these are temporary situations that should be dealt with and moved on from. Don't let pride or your ego allow them to last longer than they need to.

We should always have love to return to.

_____

_____

_____

_____

_____

277

When you have it rough, things seems to always be a struggle. Just remember, the enemy always picks those they fear the most to try and destroy. Your life has the potential for greatness, why wouldn't they want to keep you discouraged?

Rise above it all, fulfill your destiny and shame all your enemies.

278

Some of the happiest people are those who hold LOVE in high regards, some of the saddest people are those who have never learned how to love. As important as love is, you can spend a lifetime never understanding it's meaning in your life therefore,
never truly finding yourself.

LOVE is the answer.

_____

_____

_____

_____

_____

279

Know what works for you and build upon that. Watching another's success, wishing it was yours, wont move you forward unless you need a mentor, Iron sharpens iron. Never be the damp cloth to anyones flame. The more you build yourself up, the more helpful you can be to others.

Be your biggest project.

_____

_____

_____

_____

_____

280

Good and bad happen daily, what matters is what we choose to focus on. It's human nature to focus on the bad as it gets more reaction from our peers, plus our emotions are tied to sympathize or empathize with the bad. The good gets overlooked or taken for granted as if it's a given, yet when it doesn't happen we're sad. So if the good is what we need, why isn't it celebrated, appreciated or talked about more often?

We are quick to tell the world of all the bad that's done

_____

_____

_____

_____

_____

281

to us, but how many calls are made about our blessings? Even if things are tough on you be happy for the blessings others are receiving. Instead of wishing it was you, understand their success means there's still hope for you. The ones being blessed might open the doors to your blessings. Your day will come.

282

Make sure whenever you reach your breaking point, it's to break away from the things you've done to cause pain. Make your point of no return be never returning to self defeating habits. Make your rock bottom be that solid foundation needed to get started again. In others words, take ownership of all of your failures and use them as fuel to get going. Life means living, so it's forward regardless.

_____

_____

_____

_____

_____

283

We all have reasons for our actions, especially if we know they are wrong or could be perceived that way. When confronted we are quick to explain the reasons instead of accepting the truth. Defense mechanism or not, the world would be a much better place if we didn't look for reasons to defend our bad behaviors and just work on changing them.

_____

_____

_____

_____

_____

284

Anyone can be a blessing to another, it's just a matter of caring enough to not care what's in it for you. It's such a great feeling to have someone care enough to sincerely inquire if you are okay. I've come to realize that some of the greatest gifts don't cost the giver anything but their time to care.

_____

_____

_____

_____

_____

285

It's funny how quickly we adapt to changes in life as humans, couple days of severe cold weather and 25 degrees can feel like summer. A string of setbacks can make one easily appreciate the little they took for granted. Thank our winters don't last forever.

_____

_____

_____

_____

_____

286

Never have "ungrateful amnesia" where you end up forgetting those who were there for you in your time of need. Often times we end up forgetting those that stood with us through our trials, taking them for granted while celebrating our victories. Always remember everyone that played a role in your victories, even if you can't pay them all back. At least try finding ways to help others overcome as well. Pay it forward.

_____

_____

_____

_____

_____

287

It's quite clear to me that we can live a lifetime and not get all the answers to life's questions. You have the ability, however, to make your life an example for others based on integrity. Your life might be the answer others are looking for, not just the good but also the mistakes you've made.

Accept the responsibility
and teach what you've been taught.

_____

_____

_____

_____

_____

288

We all know when we've had enough and it has nothing to do with quitting or giving up. I'm talking about enough of whatever negativity we've tolerated for far too long. The problem is, we've become so accustomed to the wrong that we end up making excuses for it. Wrong is wrong and enough is enough.

It's up to you to free yourself.

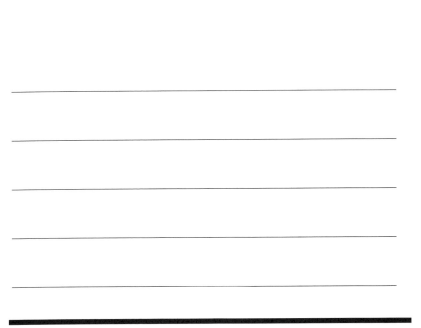

<u>289</u>

If we can humble ourselves enough to be viewed through a mirror of honesty, our life would be much more manageable. Most of our issues lie in our disbelief of our perfection. Your truth will set you free to live more internally happy.

_____

_____

_____

_____

_____

290

Nothing ever really changes until you do. All the issues of yesterday will follow you if you don't find a way to change them. Life flows continuously around us, it's ever evolving. If we can't grab the concept that it all begins with us, our issues will remain. Don't stand in the way of your own dreams and happiness.
Let's change for the better.

_____

_____

_____

_____

_____

291

Never be so caught up with the bad experiences of the past that you cant see the good in new ones. Use the past as a lesson but also use it as a reason to expect better as you now have something to grade it by. Being hurt in the past can make you afraid of love but try not to shun it. Try to appreciate it for what it is currently. Only love can heal the wounds of the past
and make you whole again.

292

You might not agree that you're a better person because of your experiences. However, you can't deny that you're now more experienced. Wisdom unfortunately comes most of the time from going through tough things. Though you wished the "bad" never happened, you're never the same after going through trying times, the key is to identify how much stronger you are because of what you once believed was impossible to handle.

You are stronger than you think.

_____

_____

_____

_____

_____

293

I'm in love with being alive and my loving relationship extends to whomever I'm fortunate to share my daily journey of life with. We must be joyful with the special gift of life and never just take this wonderful daily opportunity for granted. Be in love with the fact that you have another chance to share love with those that mean so much to you. Love hard and ignore the things that try to distract you from understanding how precious the amazing gift of life is. Love is the key.

294

There are times in life when things happen to you beyond your wildest expectations. Others will look on in amazement saying how lucky you are. It's not luck it's a blessing. Some good seed you sowed has matured or some prayers from awhile back just got answered.

When this happens, just know you are blessed not lucky.

_____

_____

_____

_____

_____

295

Old habits die hard but if it's a habit that has caused you or someone you love pain, then you have to kill that habit. Our habits are not automatic these are things we choose to do, so in the name of love we can now choose to do different.

Just remember the last results and try not to repeat it.

_____

_____

_____

_____

_____

296

You must remember what lies within you. Too many times when the struggles of life attack, we quickly forget our past accomplishments. Our current issues always seem to cast a shadow of doubt over our abilities to achieve. Once you're alive, your success still lies within you. Have confidence in knowing you're capable of rebuilding and exceeding your past successes because you've done it all before.

297

Don't be afraid, you have all you need.
Any situation in life that you can learn from can't lead to
your demise. Once you're alive and able to learn from it,
you have the ability to live and be better from it.

Live strong through life's setbacks,
they're designed to make you stronger.

298

Sometimes it's our own expectations that become our problem. Careful of the reasons behind the bar you raise or lower to govern your life. Stay in reality and never be an enemy of your own progress.

_____

_____

_____

_____

_____

299

Life has no owners manual. What we are given from birth is exposure to environments that shape our reality. The key is with continued exposure to new things, we have the ability to change our realities. Life has no owners manual because it is a work in progress, with new chapters written everyday. Let your life story be a fun-filled autobiography and not just a sad eulogy.

300

Relationships take work. Arguments will happen but you must always have love and honesty as your foundation. It doesn't matter who is right or wrong. With love as your core you will always have a base to return to, so disagreements won't last. If it's your fault step on your ego and apologize.

Don't be afraid to be wrong sometimes.

_____

_____

_____

_____

_____

301

In most cases, you will not get rewarded for doing the right thing. We as a society don't take the time to amplify good but use loud speakers to broadcast the bad. Let's break the cycle and appreciate someone for doing the right thing so they can be encouraged to continue. Lift them up so more will join in and bring change.

_____

_____

_____

_____

_____

302

The most excruciating pain becomes easier to handle when you have loved ones there to help you through it. There is no way of measuring the healing power of LOVE. Love has a way of nurturing wounds that even doctors don't understand. Love is the all in all, it's the antidote that supersedes all other medicine.

I am so in love with those that love me because I know they're the reason I'm surviving.

303

It's better to encourage one another because none of us really have it right. Wishing others the best on their life journey is best because we need the same wishes. Time spent judging another just adds more negative energy to an already chaotic world.

_____

_____

_____

_____

_____

304

Your faith allows hope in the unseen and unknown things. Your actions allow change in the things you see and know daily. While in the physical form your actions are what determine your results.

Work to achieve. It's not just what you believe.

_____

_____

_____

_____

_____

305

It's good to have a forgiving heart but if you never address the hurt with the person how can you truly heal? Forgiveness doesn't have to mean ignoring what happened, address it, discuss it and forgive it. Too many times we think we are taking the high road when all we are doing is stacking more emotional weight.

Free yourself by speaking up.

_____

_____

_____

_____

_____

306

Being pushed beyond what you thought was possible, is a clear indication there are so many serious life situations you have no control over. The ability to adjust to whatever life throws at you is key to your survival. Never live a life so disconnected from others because at your most vulnerable points, you will need the love and support of others to make it through.

Love will see you through.

_____

_____

_____

_____

_____

307

When you are passionate about your life's purpose, you will accomplish great things. Just think about others who have lived a shorter lifespan and achieved greatness. If they did it, you can too. Don't give up on your purpose.

_____

_____

_____

_____

_____

308

In the midst of your greatest pains may lie your greatest lessons. Life is designed so that most get to the lessons or the pleasures without the pain. But guess what? That isn't always the case. Sometimes lessons are painful and difficult. Don't downplay the hard road traveled. Those details may be needed to help you along the way. Experience is the best teacher, so you will also become a better teacher based on what you've experienced.

_____

_____

_____

_____

_____

309

The measure of a person can still be defined by their actions during the toughest periods of their lives. People can always speculate about how they would behave if really bad times happened to them, but there isn't much room for preparation once you're faced with some of your worst fears as your reality.

310

Everything seems harder when you are frustrated or
angry, even the simplest task seems like a burden.
Take a moment to stop and address the source of our
frustration before we transfer it to another situation.
Things done in anger or frustration are normally
not your best so catch yourself before the regrets.

_____

_____

_____

_____

_____

311

Some of us are competitive by nature which is okay at times. However, if our need to win makes us mad at the success of others, or we try to hold someone back from succeeding, then it is time to assess. Don't allow healthy competition to turn into stinking thinking and selfishness. Real competition is only good when we are all equally matched.

_____

_____

_____

_____

_____

312

If you constantly worry about something and it becomes reality, did you help to make it happen? If there is the power of positive thinking then wouldn't the opposite be true as well? Be careful about what you focus your energy on. Try to think positive as much as you can because negative thinking may bring negative results.

_____

_____

_____

_____

_____

313

Good people still exist in the world, it's just that we are programmed as a society to focus on the negative ones. We all know people that are unsung heroes in our lives, who consistently do more good than bad. Start celebrating your heroes. The change begins with us.

_____

_____

_____

_____

_____

314

If you can't wake up everyday and find something to feel good about within yourself, it is time for a change. You need yourself at your best and that involves self-love and admiration. You may not always get it right but believe that you are someone that you can be proud of.

315

Leaning on your own understanding doesn't work for all situations. You may be convinced that you have it right and later learn that you were wrong. Don't be afraid to listen to others and check your facts when necessary. Be open to always learning.

316

Learn from those who continue to live and find happiness in the midst of their trials. For they understand that there's more to life than what they are going through. Take time to look for the brighter side within the darkness.

_____

_____

_____

_____

_____

317

Is your life the way you always imagined it? If not, what are you doing to change your circumstances? Remember, each day is the first day of the rest of your life. What you desire has been achieved before and that means you can do it as well. It's never too late.

Don't stop striving for the life you want to live.

318

Love can't be grown artificially and it can't be maintained under false pretenses. Love has to be cultivated naturally with the right ingredients. So many of us live our lives without even knowing that we don't have the real thing.

Once the eyes of your heart becomes open,
no synthetic love will do.

_____

_____

_____

_____

_____

319

It is very easy to become so consumed by your problems that you forget that there's more to life. As critical as your issues may seem, try to appreciate the simple joys of being alive. Focusing so much on the things that are wrong make you miss the many rights. It's not about ignoring your problems, it's about also recognizing your blessings. Let the good keep you going.

320

When someone trusts you with their heart, that's a precious gift that shouldn't be taken lightly. It means even when they are not around, their love source should be protected by you. When love is placed in your control, only love can protect it. Protect a heart with your heart.

It is the safest place for love.

_____

_____

_____

_____

_____

321

It's not what people say about you that's important, it's what you answer to. A person can judge you based on what they believe but only you can validate it by your actions. Be firm in who you are so that you don't fall victim to another's false definition of you.

_____

_____

_____

_____

_____

322

Sometimes close family members don't have a clue as to who you are or they are blinded by situations from the past. Love them from a distance.

Positive or negative, family is a part of who you are, so just love through it all and try to grow with them.

_____

_____

_____

_____

_____

323

Each person is responsible, for working to achieve their dreams. That doesn't mean you can't assist them along the way. You can teach, inspire, encourage or help in numerous ways. Helping someone reach their goals is one of life's greatest rewards. Once you're not infected with "stinking thinking", believing that somehow their success means your failure. Let's help each to the top.

_____

_____

_____

_____

_____

324

Any love, whether a romantic relationship or friendship, that requires no effort from you, might feel good but it's very selfish. You can be spoiled into believing it's all about you but others are busy giving while you're just taking. Life is always about balance, it's about give and take. Never be selfish in your approach to the people you need the most in your life.

_____

_____

_____

_____

_____

325

One reason to not fail or lose might be the fact that you have too many waiting to celebrate your loss or failures. Win or succeed because you refuse to have them celebrate.

Celebrate with those you know mean you well and keep working hard on crushing the hater's expectations.

_____

_____

_____

_____

_____

326

It is sometimes painful when someone you love and trust disappoints you with actions that prove they don't know you. Your love isn't always enough to protect you from the flaws of others.

Jealousy, hate, envy and greed may still exist in those you love. Love without expectation because it won't always be returned in the same way that it's given.

_____

_____

_____

_____

_____

327

Be a person of strong character. Know what it is you stand for and don't waver. Too many times we compromise for acceptance and end up losing ourselves in the process. Stay true to who you are because if you don't then you are lying to the rest of the world by pretending to be what you are not and most importantly, you are lying to yourself. Free yourself by being yourself.

_____

_____

_____

_____

_____

328

We are all just searching for answers to life's questions, but don't let the quest overshadow your ability to enjoy life itself. Wisdom comes from us being students of life while we are living it. No one knows it all.

_____

_____

_____

_____

_____

329

Find things in life to use as reminders to remain humble. Life is filled with ups and downs but you must remember the downs when you're up. Too often we become caught up in our current situations we forget the struggles we went through to get there. Always remain humble.

_____

_____

_____

_____

_____

330

It's hard to wish good for others or even be truly happy for them when you are struggling. We have to break that mindset and understand that one making it gives you hope that your breakthrough is possible and next. Success breeds success so lets celebrate one another.

_____

_____

_____

_____

_____

331

Don't use the fact that some things might be bad right now to get into more trouble. It's easy to make things worse by using the bad as an excuse. Finding a solution to one problem is far easier than trying to clean up the mess you made by being additionally reckless.
Bad is only bad until you make it worse.

_____

_____

_____

_____

_____

332

You can't be a control freak in every area of your life. It's impossible for you to control the actions of others that are connected to your life. Learn to not be frustrated when others do what's in their best interest. Just like you would adjust to unexpected weather, adjust accordingly to unexpected life events and keep it moving.

_____

_____

_____

_____

_____

333

You should never look at yourself as negative when you still have the ability to learn and change. You're twice defeated when you're viewing your life lessons as failures instead of opportunities to get better. If you see yourself as negative, the rest of the world will follow.

334

Finding comfort in who you are is sometimes easier said than done. Society frowns upon those who make an effort to go against what is considered "normal". People never like your bravery when they believe it challenges their cowardice. Being honest or true to yourself in a world of pretenders just trying to fit in, isn't easy but it grants you the freedom to be who you want to be.

_____

_____

_____

_____

_____

335

There are many gifts that lie within you but there is one that is the truest essence of who you are. You must identify what it is. Once you identify it, the gift must be nurtured and developed so that you are able to fulfill your purpose. Don't shy away from your calling. Give of your gift whenever asked upon by others who recognize that talent that is uniquely within you.

Your gift is directly connected to your happiness.

_____

_____

_____

_____

_____

336

In the beginning, your heart makes you do things for others in order to gain their love and attention. Then, once you have them, complacency takes over and we start taking them for granted. If we could maintain some of the things that nurtured the love in the beginning, then the love would stay fresh and alive.

_____

_____

_____

_____

_____

337

Love needs your attention to flourish.
Rekindle the spark by remembering how it all began.
If your life has become too routine, that you feel like a
bystander in your own story, it is time for a change. True
living involves you being an active decision maker in your
own life. Going with the flow, is just like giving up.
Stop being a walking dead, start living every day.

_____

_____

_____

_____

_____

338

Life isn't about always trying to win a popularity contest. Your quality of life shouldn't be based on the quantity of people that surround you. Love those around you so strongly so that your lives will be so filled with great memories to last a lifetime. It's better to have tons of memories with a few than few memories with a ton.

_____

_____

_____

_____

_____

339

Our fear often-times becomes our reality based solely on focus. When we put too much focus on our fears, we can will them into existence. Be careful about the things you spend your time focusing on, your energy has the ability to make them reality. Keep it positive.

340

Know your support crew. The ones that are there and have always been there. It is so comforting to know they are there allowing you to still act strong in times of weakness. Even if it's just one person that has your back, love them with all you've got because they love you for you and stand beside you no matter what.

_____

_____

_____

_____

_____

341

What choices have you made to contribute to your own unhappiness? Too many times we choose to be unhappy by focusing on the negatives and doing things we know lead to sorrow. Being happy requires us to make hard choices about who we are and what we are looking for. Do the choices you make have your best interest in mind?

342

Try to pay less attention to those unhappy about your success and more attention to the ones who genuinely celebrate your blessings with you. There will be those who believe that you doing good makes them look bad. What's more amazing though, is those that can see your efforts and celebrate the fact that you have earned your results. Life isn't about comparing, it's about compassion and caring.

_____

_____

_____

_____

_____

343

Learning to recognize my blessings and truly appreciate them has been one of life greatest joys. Identifying your talents and getting the opportunity to learn and master them brings fulfillment to the soul. The gift of life is meant to be opened and enjoyed.

_____

_____

_____

_____

_____

344

You must be serious enough about life to want to make a difference. It's not good enough to float through, not rocking the boat and refusing to stand up for your core beliefs. Being a part of a passive majority only allows the aggressive minority to continue leading us into chaos.

_____

_____

_____

_____

_____

345

Ignorance continues because some refuse to share the things we've learned. It also continues because we all refuse to acknowledge our own ignorance.

Change will never come through staying comfortable in our own ignorance. We must seek the knowledge and spread it.

_____

_____

_____

_____

_____

346

It's truly difficult to take a leap of faith when there are so many obstacles distracting you from the jump. Having dreams don't mean much if you can't visualize them as your reality. Having people that encourage your dreams, who recognize your potential and support your dreams is all the push you need to soar.

Bless up the dream builders.

_____

_____

_____

_____

_____

347

I've never lived until I found love, I've never loved until I found my reason to live. Life is nothing without love and love is nothing without lives to love. I'm an extension of the love that exist so therefore I only exist because of love.

_____

_____

_____

_____

_____

348

Sometimes you have a chance to correct a mistake quickly, it doesn't stop what happened but it allows you to soften the impact. You can't change what's already done but you can always work hard to prevent things from reoccurring. Correct quickly while learning how to stop having to apologize.

_____

_____

_____

_____

_____

349

The never ending cycle of trying to survive can be overwhelming. The vicious cycle creates short lived moments of happiness which are often overshadowed by the strenuous pressure of trying to keep afloat. Oftentimes we create the pressure cooker environment by living beyond our means without ever realizing we are over extending ourselves.

_____

_____

_____

_____

_____

350

Never downplay a good support system. Having people in your corner that don't just understand what you're going through, but also make an active effort in finding solutions makes a huge difference. Pain intensifies when problems occur and you feel like you're all alone.

Having someone there
in times of despair
for those that care
is like an abundance of fresh air.

_____

_____

_____

_____

_____

351

Life can seem meaningless if we are only living from problem to problem. What is the purpose of existing until the next issue without seeing any bright side? Truth be told, life is filled with an abundance of positivity between each problem that occurs.

When we only choose to see the bad,
the good is always missed.

_____

_____

_____

_____

_____

352

If you think you've arrived at a level where you can now look scornfully down at others, then you didn't really pay attention to your journey.

Life will prepare you for each position but personal perceptions will determine your true success.

353

There is certain pain you feel when someone you truly love disappoints you with their actions. It's hard to understand how their love could be so blind to your feelings. You can't control anyone's actions but it would be nice if others didn't see love through selfish eyes.

_____

_____

_____

_____

_____

354

Not all that glitters is gold but some things actually are. Don't allow past experiences or personal biases make you miss out on people or situations that are actually golden. Take each situation as they come, optimistically attentive while using history only as protective boundaries, not decision makers.

355

If we can't recognize how blessed we are then we will never truly be able to reap the benefits of our blessings.

_____

_____

_____

_____

_____

356

If you're thinking, why is everyone else able to "do" and I'm not?, Maybe you're just not living up to your own expectations of your potential. No one can do what you're capable of doing but you, in the same way no one living their best life can ever stop you from living yours.

Stop watching and get in the darn game.

_____

_____

_____

_____

_____

357

Sometimes we stress simply because we care so much. Even though we know stressing doesn't help, we are still concerned about the end results. Even the things we have control over can be mismanaged and cause stress to happen. Stress is the negative part in the balance of life.

_____

_____

_____

_____

_____

358

Maturity is understanding that just because you can doesn't mean that you have to. We all have the ability to be reckless, it's our choice not to act on those feelings. Hold yourself accountable enough to mentally stay in a controlled environment.

359

Issues in your past you didn't properly deal with, are like wounds with thin scabs that can open back up with the slightest impact and hurt just like the first time.

You must address your emotional wounds and allow them proper healing time before any rigid exposure ends up causing severe pain.

_____

_____

_____

_____

_____

360

Being stuck in your ways doesn't equate to growth. Regardless of how old you are there should be room left for improvement. Accepting your behaviors that offend others as your norm is selfish. Never expect anything from others that you're not willing to give of yourself.

_____

_____

_____

_____

_____

361

It's okay to do the things that makes you happy while also making those that love you proud. Too often we feel guilty for being happy because of others who may be in a worse situation. But if someone truly loves you, they will be happy that you're happy.

Love never blocks the path to happiness because love isn't selfish.

_____

_____

_____

_____

_____

362

Energy and the mind are very powerful. There are some people whose energy will always clash with yours and no matter how hard you try, things always seem to result in conflict. Learn how to control your reactions towards them by understanding that your actions are something you will always have control over. You are not meant to share energy with everyone.

_____

_____

_____

_____

_____

363

Don't waste your tears. Only use them when you're truly full of hurtful poison inside and you use your tears as a release. Use your other powers, such as love, laughter, friends & family, hobbies, meditation and affirmations as a means to cope with it all.

Turn your sad tears into tears of joy.

364

Your actions are only routine to the uninformed eyes.
Those that really know you know the effort you put in
daily to make things happen. Your efforts are for you to
know and for others to figure out by judging wrongfully.
They think they know but they have no idea.

_____

_____

_____

_____

_____

365

It's so strange how we forget how bad it feels to be treated unfairly when it's being done to someone else. We can be very selfish sometimes with our compassion, it shouldn't only matter when it's happening to you. Right is right and wrong is wrong regardless.

_____

_____

_____

_____

_____

Made in the USA
Middletown, DE
19 February 2019